COMPUTERS

MAKING

CONTACT

Published by Smart Apple Media
123 South Broad Street
Mankato, Minnesota 56001

Photos: page 8–CORBIS/Bettmann; page 9–CORBIS;
page 10–CORBIS/Jerry Cooke; page 16–CORBIS/Ed
Eckstein; page 23–CORBIS/Ted Spiegel

Design and Production: EvansDay Design

Library of Congress Cataloging-in-Publication Data
Gibson, Diane, 1966–
Computers / by Diane Gibson
p. cm. – (Making contact)
Includes index.
Summary: Examines the history, operations, termi-
nology, and uses of computers and describes the
different kinds.
ISBN 1-887068-60-0
1. Computers—Juvenile literature. [1. Computers.]
I. Title. II. Series: Making contact (Mankato, Minn.)

QA76.23.R54   1999
004—dc21   98-30293

First edition

9 8 7 6 5 4 3 2 1

COMPUTERS

MAKING

CONTACT

DIANE GIBSON

IF ALL THE COMPUTERS IN THE world suddenly disappeared, humanity would be thrown into chaos. Traffic lights wouldn't work. Most cars would stop running. Video games, television, and the Internet would be out of commission. Hospitals and businesses all over the world would have to shut down. Space shuttles could not leave Earth. This book and millions of others would not exist without computers, which help people to write, design, edit, and print. Computers have become so integrated into almost every aspect of our lives that we often take them for granted. However, their roles in science, transportation, business, and many other areas make them an essential part of our world.

From Beads to Microchips

By definition, a computer is something that computes, or does math. It is a highly sophisticated calculator, a device that performs mathematical functions. Human fingers are a type of calculating device too, since people sometimes use them to add and subtract. This is why  fingers are also known as digits (another word for numbers). The human brain is the ultimate computer, capable of adding, subtracting, multiplying, dividing, and performing many other functions of logic.

In 1694, a German mathematician named Gottfried Leibniz studied Blaise Pascal's calculating device. By rearranging the gears and wheels, Leibniz discovered that the machine could perform multiplication and division as well as addition and subtraction.

The first device used as a calculator, an **abacus**, was created sometime around the year 500 B.C. in Asia. An abacus usually consists of a wooden frame that holds beads strung on wires or rods. It is one of the simplest tools for performing addition. Until the 1600s, it was also the fastest tool. Even though the abacus is outdated, people in some parts of the world still use it.

In 1642, French scientist and mathematician Blaise Pascal invented the world's first automatic adding machine. Pascal's adding machine, which was created for his father's business, used wheels instead of beads, and it could perform subtraction as well as addition.

ABACUS

*a counting device that consists
of a wooden frame containing
beads strung on rods*

7

✳ THE ABACUS, THE WORLD'S FIRST CALCULATOR, WAS INVENTED ABOUT 2,500 YEARS AGO.

Each wheel had numbered notches, and each notch represented a number between 0 and 9. The first wheel represented the single digits, the second represented tens, the third represented hundreds, and so on. When the first wheel moved 10 notches, a gear automatically moved the second wheel one notch. Pascal's system proved to be a fast and efficient way to perform calculations. Today, the odometers, or mileage counters, in modern cars work in much the same way.

The next step in computer development came in 1801 when a Frenchman named Joseph Jacquard invented a way to improve the fabrics he made with a loom. Jacquard punched a pattern of holes into paper cards and placed them between the

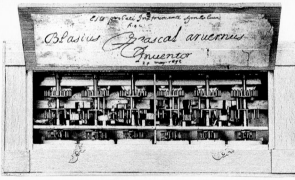

8

* BLAISE PASCAL AND HIS LANDMARK INVENTION, THE FIRST AUTOMATIC ADDING MACHINE.

rising needles and the thread on the machine. His cards then "instructed" the loom: if a needle found a hole when it rose, it passed through and made a stitch; if there was no hole, the needle was blocked. Jacquard's improved loom could create impressive woven fabrics. It was not a real computer, because it didn't actually count anything, but it gave other inventors great ideas.

Some of those ideas led to the development of modern computers. The idea for computers originally came in the 1830s from a British inventor named Charles Babbage. He spent 40 years designing a

In 1934, Dave Packard and Bill Hewlett went on a camping trip in Colorado. There the two became good friends and decided to start a business together. The name of the company, Hewlett-Packard, was decided by a coin toss. The winner, Hewlett, got top billing.

9

* JOSEPH JACQUARD, WHO MODIFIED PASCAL'S ADDING MACHINE TO CREATE A FABRIC-WEAVING DEVICE.

machine he called the analytical engine. The engine would use stored, punched cards to remember **data** and instructions, allowing people to enter mathematical problems into the machine. By following instructions on the cards, the machine would then print out the answers. In theory, the analytical engine would basically do everything a modern computer does.

Unfortunately, Babbage was way ahead of his time—the devices he needed to create his computer hadn't even been invented yet. Babbage had been dead for more than 60 years by the time scientists and mathematicians came to realize what a genius he had been.

Computers in the early 1900s were large, some filling an entire room. They were also unreliable. The ma-

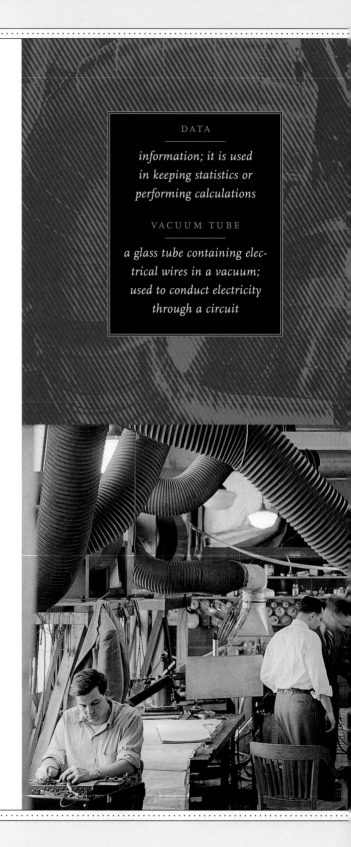

DATA

information; it is used in keeping statistics or performing calculations

VACUUM TUBE

a glass tube containing electrical wires in a vacuum; used to conduct electricity through a circuit

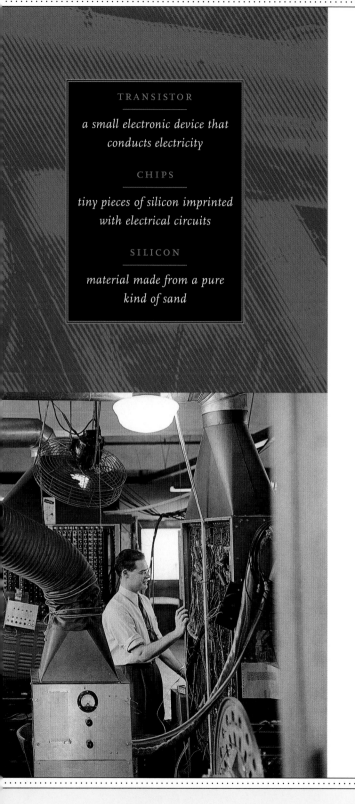

TRANSISTOR
___

a small electronic device that conducts electricity

CHIPS
___

tiny pieces of silicon imprinted with electrical circuits

SILICON
___

material made from a pure kind of sand

chines operated with the help of glass **vacuum tubes** that often overheated or broke. In many cases, the fragile vacuum tubes heated up so fast that they "blew" almost every seven minutes.

Transistors replaced vacuum tubes during the 1950s. Both devices moved electrical signals through a circuit, but transistors didn't overheat. The development of transistors, which are much smaller and longer-lasting than vacuum tubes, paved the way for today's compact computers.

The next breakthrough came in the 1960s with the invention of silicon **chips**. To make a chip, workers cut thin slices of **silicon** in a dust-free environment. Workers and visitors are actually vacuumed before entering the workroom so that it remains dust-free. The circuits that make the chip work

✳ COMPUTERS IN THE FIRST HALF OF THE 20TH CENTURY WERE ENORMOUS AND UNRELIABLE MACHINES.

are designed on a computer, then reduced in size to fit onto the tiny chip. After that, the circuits are imprinted on the silicon and baked in a furnace at about 1,830 degrees Fahrenheit (1,000° C). The chips go through this process several times until all of the circuits have been placed on the tiny surface. Once finished, the chips are cut with a laser and placed in a plastic case.

Many chips are so small that they can fit through the eye of a needle. Some, called microchips, are no bigger than a flake of pepper. These are the chips that make modern computers so small but powerful.

✳ A VACUUM TUBE, SCIENTISTS' FIRST MEANS OF SENDING ELECTRICITY THROUGH COMPUTERS.

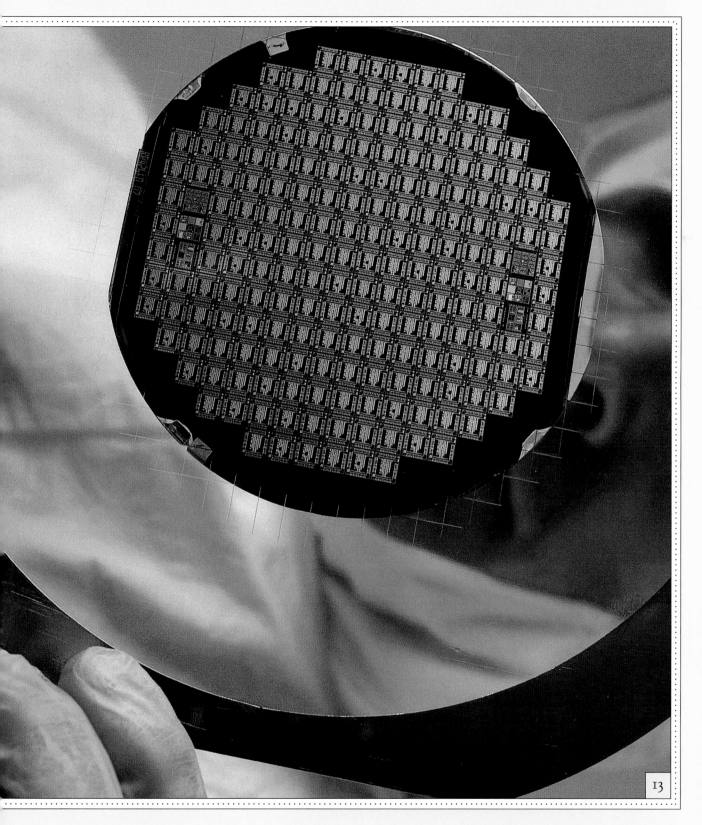

✳ A CLOSE VIEW OF A SILICON CHIP AND ITS TINY ELECTRICAL CIRCUITS.

Kinds of Computers

There are two general kinds of computers—analog and digital. Analog computers, which were used by scientists in the 1950s and 1960s, are quickly being replaced by digital computers. An analog monitors things that constantly change, such as temperature.

Chemical plants sometimes use this type of computer to watch for pressure changes and to send the proper amounts of electricity to chemical processors. The speedometer in a car is a type of analog computer, keeping track of constantly changing speeds and displaying them to the driver.

Digital computers are more familiar to today's computer users. These computers fall into one of three categories: embedded, personal, or mainframe. Almost all embedded computers are **microprocessors**, which means they are designed to control a machine. Microprocessors are components of larger products. Embedded computers are built into cars, telephones, VCRs, digital watches, and many other machines and appliances.

A personal computer is used by one person at a time. This type of computer fits on a desktop and is often used to play games, write

American scientists William Shockley, Walter Brattain, and John Bardeen developed the transistor in 1948. Their discovery replaced vacuum tubes in computers, making the machines smaller, faster, and much more reliable.

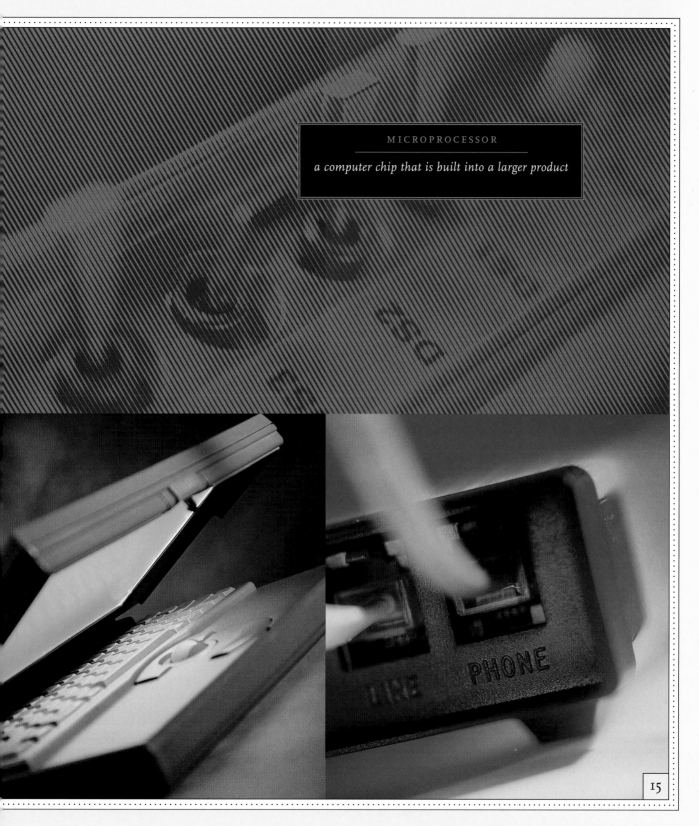

MICROPROCESSOR

a computer chip that is built into a larger product

✳ PERSONAL COMPUTERS AND MODEMS MAKE GLOBAL ELECTRONIC COMMUNICATION EASY.

letters, or connect to the Internet. Many businesses also use them to keep track of accounts and inventories. Most modern personal computers contain **modems**, which allow users to communicate with other computer users anywhere in the world.

Some personal computers are small and portable, allowing users to take them along as they travel. A laptop, one type of portable personal computer, gets its name from the fact that it is small enough to fit on a person's lap. Another type of portable computer, called a notebook, is about the same size as a looseleaf notebook.

Mainframe computers are large, powerful machines; some modern mainframes take up one or two entire rooms. Unlike older computers of similar size, these mainframes can solve

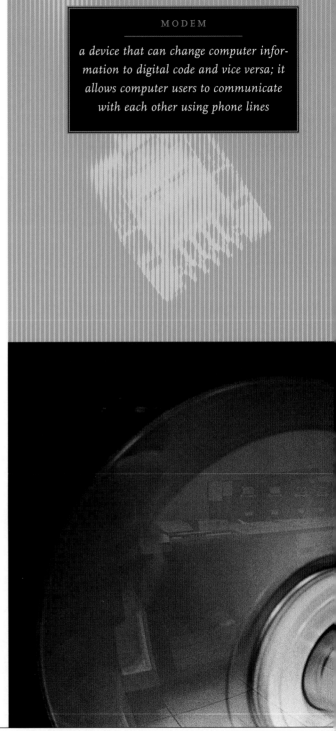

extremely complicated problems and store huge amounts of information. People can use a mainframe computer through a **dumb terminal**—a keyboard and monitor linked to the mainframe. Dumb terminals have no memory or processors, so they cannot operate if the link is broken. Hundreds of people can use these terminals and **log on** to a mainframe computer at the same time.

Supercomputers are a type of mainframe. They are the fastest, most expensive computers in the world. Scientists and engineers use them to perform such tasks as designing large aircraft, including spacecraft, and creating models of weather systems.

Seymour Cray founded Cray Research in 1972. Today, Cray's supercomputers provide computerized weather reports on television, help engineers design and build new cars, and control robots used to clean up hazardous waste sites.

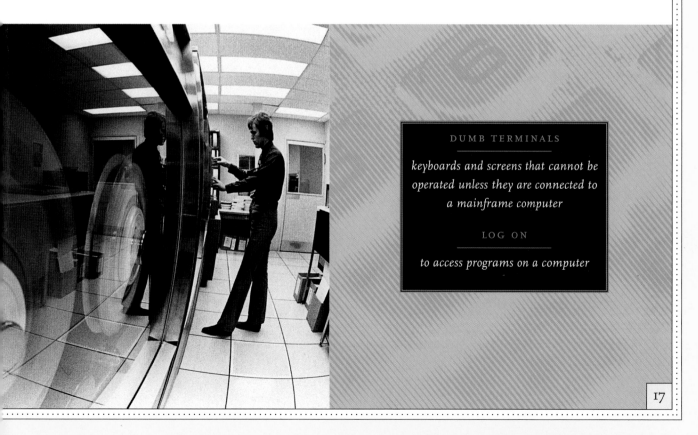

DUMB TERMINALS

keyboards and screens that cannot be operated unless they are connected to a mainframe computer

LOG ON

to access programs on a computer

＊ A MAINFRAME, THE MOST POWERFUL AND SOPHISTICATED TYPE OF COMPUTER IN THE WORLD.

Computers and people don't speak the same language. If a person types the number 17 on a keyboard, the computer will not know how to read it until the number goes through circuits to the silicon chips. In the chips, the

keyboard information is translated into a special language that the computer understands. This language, called **binary code**, is based on two numbers: 1 and 0. The computer cannot understand the number 17—or anything else in human language—without a translation.

The easiest way to understand binary code is to picture a group of doubled numbers. The first number is 1. The second number is double the first number, or 2, which is followed by 4, 8, 16, and so on; the numbers can be doubled as many times as necessary. The doubled numbers are arranged from right to left, with the highest number on the left. Five doubled numbers arranged in this manner look like this: 16 8 4 2 1.

A computer reads keyboard messages by sending electric pulses through the chips, which translate the messages into binary code. The pulses are like a light being switched on and off. A 1 indicates

Bill Gates and classmate Paul Allen founded Microsoft, the world leader in manufacturing computer software, in April 1975. The company's goal, from its founding to today, has been to create software that is fun and easy to use in both the home and office.

19

* HUMAN LANGUAGE, TAPPED OUT ON A KEYBOARD, IS QUICKLY TRANSLATED INTO BINARY CODE INSIDE COMPUTERS.

that the light is turned on; 0 means the light is turned off. A computer reads only the "on" pulses that represent the number 1. It sees the number 17 as:

16	8	4	2	1
1	0	0	0	1

The switch is "on" under the numbers 16 and 1, so the computer sees these numbers in its own language. It adds the two numbers and reads them as 17. This translation process may seem to be a lot of work, but a computer can translate human language into binary code in an instant.

Each of the digits in binary code is called a **bit**, a shortened way of saying "binary digit." Eight bits make up one **byte**. A computer with a 64-kilobyte (64K) memory can store 64,000 bytes—512,000 bits—of information.

BIT

one digit in the binary code; the smallest piece of information a computer can understand

BYTE

eight bits of information; refers to the memory capacity of a computer or disk

* Programming languages instruct computers on how to handle information.

A computer with one **megabyte** of memory can store about one million letters, numbers, and symbols.

Computers cannot follow instructions without a **programming language**. There are several languages in existence; users choose the one that best meets their needs. The computer uses special programs called compilers and assemblers to translate the programming language into binary code. Users can program a computer directly using binary code, but it is a time-consuming process. Most prefer to use a programming language and let the computer do the work.

One of the most common programming languages is BASIC (Beginner's All-purpose Symbolic Instruction Code.) This easy-to-learn language is the program taught

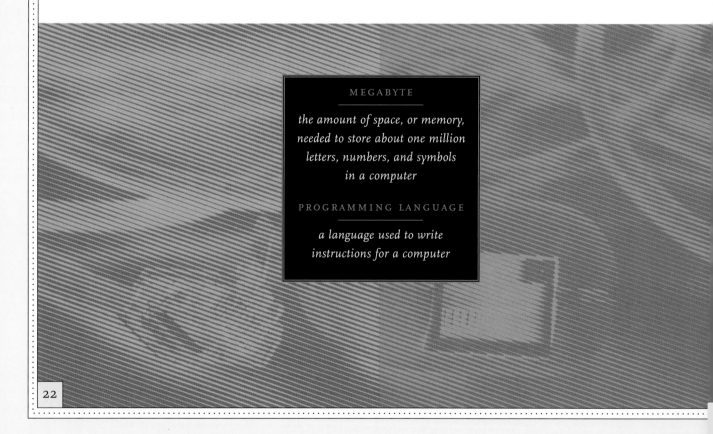

MEGABYTE
_____

*the amount of space, or memory,
needed to store about one million
letters, numbers, and symbols
in a computer*

PROGRAMMING LANGUAGE
_____

*a language used to write
instructions for a computer*

most often in schools. Languages written for businesses include COBOL (COmmon Business Oriented Language) and APL (A Programming Language). A mathematician might use a computer programmed in FORTRAN (FORmula TRANslation) to solve complicated mathematical problems.

Average users rarely program their own computers. Most people buy a programming language **software** package from a store. These software packages are different from **hardware**, which includes the computer's operating equipment: the printer, monitor, sound cards, and so on. Essentially, any part of a computer other than a disk or a software program is hardware.

> SOFTWARE
> ———
> *computer programs*
>
> HARDWARE
> ———
> *all the operating parts of a computer except software programs and computer disks*

23

✳ A COMPUTER'S HARDWARE—INCLUDING ITS KEYBOARD AND PRINTER—
ALLOW USERS TO INTERACT WITH THE MACHINE.

Input, Output, and Memory

Today's computers come in many sizes, ranging from the tiny embedded computers of a digital watch to the huge mainframes used by engineers. Computers also perform a wide range of functions. They run computer games, store huge amounts of information, and solve mathematical problems. One thing all computers have in common is the way that they work. Their operation can be divided into three steps: entering data, processing data, and producing **output**.

Any information entered into a computer is called **input**. There are many devices that allow people to enter data in a computer; the most common one is the keyboard. Another way to enter data is by using a **mouse** to input commands and manipulate information. Rolling a mouse across a surface moves a pointer on the computer screen in a corresponding direction. A user tells the computer what to do next by pointing to an on-screen word, or to a symbol called an **icon**, and clicking a button on the mouse.

Compaq Computer Corporation was started in 1981 by engineers Joseph Canion, Jim Harris, and Bill Murto. They designed their first computer on a napkin while they sat in a restaurant. By 1994, Compaq had become the world leader in personal computer manufacturing.

OUTPUT

any information a computer gives out

INPUT

any information entered into a computer

MOUSE

_a small input device used to
move the cursor or pointer
around on a computer screen_

ICON

a picture or symbol

25

※ CABLE CONNECTIONS ALLOW COMPUTERS TO STORE, PRINT, OR SEND INFORMATION THAT IS OFTEN ENTERED ON DISKS.

Modems and **disk drives** also allow input. Many people use scanners to copy pages of text or artwork and load these pages into their computers. Some users actually talk to their computers with voice activators that translate spoken language into written words. Scanners and voice activators are both types of input devices.

After a user puts information into a computer, the information goes to the **CPU**, or **Central Processing Unit**, where it is translated into binary code and sent to the appropriate part of the computer. It may be stored in the computer's memory or processed to solve a problem. If the user needs an answer or analysis from the computer, the requested information returns to the CPU. It is then translated into human language and sent to an

DISK DRIVE

a machine that reads from computer disks and writes on them

CPU (CENTRAL PROCESSING UNIT)

the control center of a computer

26

output device. In most cases, this entire process is done within a few seconds.

Many input devices are also used for output. For example, a disk drive reads data from a disk, but it can also copy data onto a blank disk. A modem brings information into a user's computer, but it can also send information to other computers. Printers, monitors, and speakers are among the other main output devices.

Computers can store memory at any time during their operation. There are two basic types of memory: **ROM** and **RAM**. ROM, which means Read Only Memory, consists of permanent instruction files that are built into the computer. ROM files can be read only—users cannot erase or write over them. If the machine is turned off or unplugged, the ROM files are not lost.

RAM stands for Random Access Memory. These memory files hold all the information a computer receives while it is operating. The files also store information the computer generates during calculations. The data contained on RAM files is not permanent—users can erase or replace this data. When the computer is turned off or unplugged, any memory that is not "saved" disappears.

The best-selling computer in history is the Commodore 64. Introduced in 1982, it came with 64K RAM and a sound synthesizer chip. Commodore International sold 22 million of these computers in 1983, then went out of business in 1994.

ROM (Read Only Memory)	RAM (Random Access Memory)
the built-in part of a computer's memory that stores permanent information	*temporary memory storage in a computer*

Computers are more than machines that sit on desks. They make up an important technology that extends to many aspects of our everyday lives. In fact, computers are helpful in more ways than most people realize.

For example, household appliances often contain programmed microchips that tell the machines how to operate. These chips tell refrigerators how cold the food inside should be kept. They tell clothes dryers when the drying cycle is finished.

In most grocery stores, each item has its own bar code, a pattern of bars or numbers that can be read by a computer. Cashiers scan this code with a laser, which sends information to a computerized cash register that adds up the shopper's purchases. When all the bar codes have been scanned and added, the computer prints an itemized receipt. Some shoppers pay for their groceries with a check card that authorizes a computer to take the money out of their bank accounts.

Many people use computerized security systems to protect their homes from intruders. Computers can also turn lights on and off at programmed times or automatically water lawns. The U.S. Postal Service uses computers to provide better and faster mail delivery. Almost everything people read today—newspapers, magazines,

In 1997, Intel developed the 7.5 million-transistor Pentium® II processor. This leap in computer technology let people send photos and video over the Internet at faster speeds and with greater clarity than ever before. It also allowed consumers to expertly edit their own home movies.

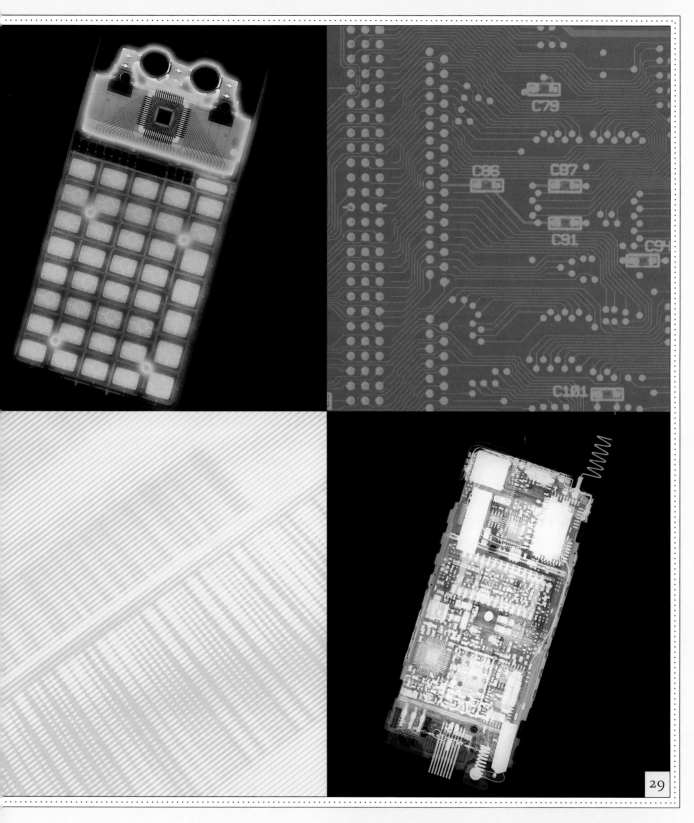

✳ X-RAY IMAGES OF A CELLULAR PHONE AND AN ADDING MACHINE SHOW THE COMPLEX
ARRANGEMENT OF INTERNAL COMPUTERS.

and books—is printed with the help of computers. Computer users can even read many newspapers on the Internet.

It's impossible to predict what computers of the future will be able to do. Their uses and capabilities will be limited only by human imagination. One thing is a certainty, however: computers of the future will be smaller, faster, and more powerful than any of today's computers. Such changes will inevitably lead to advances in space exploration, medical technology, transportation, and more. With each new development in this field of technology, people's lives will become easier and more efficient.

In 1998, National Semiconductor built a microchip smaller than a flake of coarse pepper. Cellular phones can use as many as 50 of these chips. An equally powerful phone made with the old vacuum tubes would be larger than the Washington Monument.

31

* COMPUTERS—THE ONGOING RESULTS OF DECADES OF HUMAN THOUGHT—WILL CONTINUE TO CHANGE THE WORLD.

I N D E X

A
abacus 6, 7
adding machines 6–8, 29
Allen, Paul 18
analog computers 14
analytical engine 10
automobiles 5, 14, 17

B
Babbage, Charles 9–10
bar codes 28–30
Bardeen, John 14
binary code 18–20, 22
bits 20–22
Brattain, Walter 14
bytes 20–22
   megabytes 22

C
Canion, Joseph 24
Commodore 64 27
Compaq Computer Corporation 24
Cray, Seymour 17

D
digital computers 14–17

E
Electronic Numerical Integrator and
      Calculator (ENIAC) 12
embedded computers 14

G
Gates, Bill 18

H
hardware 23, 24–27
Harris, Jim 24
Hewlett, Bill 9
Hewlett-Packard 9

I
Intel 28
Internet 5, 28, 30

J
Jacquard, Joseph 8–9

L
Leibniz, Gottfried 6

M
mainframe computers 14, 16–17
   dumb terminals 17
   supercomputers 17
microprocessors 14, 15
Microsoft 18
modems 16
Murto, Bill 24

N
National Semiconductor 30

P
Packard, Dave 9
Pascal, Blaise 6–8
personal computers 14–16
   laptop 16
   notebook 16
programming languages 21, 22–23
punchcards 8–9, 10

R
Random Access Memory (RAM)
      26, 27
Read Only Memory (ROM) 27

S
Shockley, William 14
silicon chips 11–12, 13, 18–20
   microchips 12, 28, 30
software packages 23

T
telephones 14, 30
transistors 11, 14, 28

V
vacuum tubes 10, 11, 12, 14, 30